REVEALED WAYS OF GOD

Healing a broken heart &
Saving a crushed spirit

Hezekiel Mshitiseng Mashego

Revealed Ways of God

REVEALED WAYS OF GOD

Healing a broken heart &
Saving a crushed spirit

Hezekiel Mshitiseng Mashego

Matlateng Publishers

Pretoria

Copyright © 2020 @Hezekiel M Mashego

All rights reserved.

No part of this book may be reproduced or transmitted in any form or by any means, electronic or mechanical, including photocopying, recording, or by any information storage and retrieval system, without permission in writing from the copyright owner.

All scripture quotations are derived from the Holy Bible unless otherwise indicated.

Edited by Ntombezinhle Ngidi (Book Connection Editors)
Cover Design & Layout by Aubrey Zesh (Creative Books)

Published by:

Matlateng Publishers (Pty) Ltd
PO Box 296
La Montagne
Pretoria
0184

Email: Info@matlatengpublishers.co.za

ISBN 978-0-620-90012-6

"…teach me your ways so I may know you and continue to find favour with you" (Exodus 33:13).

FOREWORD

An insightful read in many ways that I feel will help many who will read it. One of the greatest takeaways from this book is its embrace of God's grace and His favour. Mr Hezekiel Mshitiseng Mashego outlines that tragedies cannot mean that God is absent or out of control.

Whether you are dealing with life trials; temptations; loss of loved one/s; loss of a job or loss of faith, "Revealed Ways of God" offers you a message of heartfelt hope. You will not find answers to the stresses and problems of life in tranquillizers and stimulants but in a profound understanding and application of relevant scriptural principles.

Mr Mashego probes the purposes of suffering offers bible based references that reveal the ways of God. He delineates how to join hands with God in prayer and faith to discern His will in all your life challenges.

He explains that if we embrace our challenges in the right ways, we can discover a contagious joy that

Revealed Ways of God

will magnify Jesus' grace in the eyes of the watching world. "Revealed Ways of God" has great testimonies to reference how God can handle the questions, doubts, fears and pain in the lives of ordinary people.

If you have ever wondered where you need to go in life during those times when the road ahead seems so uncertain, you will learn how God's hand can guide you through, even to places you wouldn't have otherwise reached. You can learn to see things from God's perspective.

He understands the pitfall of pain as well as the heavenly heights of spirit-based joy. Gripping stories from the bible are used in the book to show how God uses life trials for our own good. "Revealed Ways of God" is biblically grounded; respectfully honest and of practical wisdom.

Mr Mashego has personal experiences of being plunged into the life's abyss. Using his life experiences of staggering loss and soaring hope, he takes the reader on a journey of pain straight to the heart of God. Your broken heart is precious to God and he cares about your struggles. Mr Mashego implores us to place our trust in Him and rest as we wait His plan to unfold in our lives.

---Eva Molotsi---

PREFACE

A desire for writing this book was inspired and driven by unconditional love for God and His work, especially sharing God's word with His children to understand His ways and know Him better to continue finding favour.

After serving for more than twenty years in the ministry, caring for many souls; some facing difficult challenges and unbearable painful losses, in some instances, they would lose hope and think of giving up in life. The intervention through God's word would really make a difference to strengthen their faith and revive their hope.

I also went through several unbearable painful losses in my lifetime. Despite the agonising loses, I have been steadfast in my faith and kept on trusting God. Truly, He's been always appearing in all situations and I'm still living a fulfilling joyful life covered by the peace of Christ.

I conceived the idea of writing an inspirational book about five years ago. I started the write up slowly and taking some breaks in between. It took about seven months with full commitment to finish the book and get it ready for publishing.

The aim of this book is to serve as an extended platform of sharing God's word with many of His children. The book has chapters covering unbearable painful loses that can leave you with a broken heart and a crushed spirit, a chapter of life restoration and the last chapter covers a fulfilling life after going through challenges, failures and victories.

The book can be read by those who went through a painful loss, anyone with a family member or friend who went through the loss to offer support by providing encouragement and anyone who has not yet gone through the painful loss to get an understanding about the pain that others go through.

ACKNOWLEDGEMENTS

First and foremost, I would like to thank the loving, caring and gracious heavenly Father who has revealed His ways throughout my journey of faith and also for inspiring me to write and complete this book. I would like to pay my sincere gratitude to everyone who has been part of my life throughout my journey of faith:

I must thank my beloved family, for being loving and supportive, especially in assisting with the content review of this book. Their contribution was so amazing.

I must also thank my dear brothers and sisters in Christ I fellowship with in the house of the Lord. I thank their love and support in all circumstances.

I owe my gratitude to my cousins, Musa Mazibuko and Luki Matsabe for encouraging me to write books. Surely, God has specially used them to open my eyes and realise the potential.

Finally, I pay my sincere gratitude to Ntombezinhle Ngidi, the Editor and Aubrey Zesh, the Graphic Designer and Sello Phoshoko who played a part in publishing, they have done a sterling job for the accomplishment of this book that will be food for soul across the global village.

CONTENTS

FOREWORD vii

PREFACE ix

ACKNOWLEDGEMENTS xi

INTRODUCTION 1

LIFE WITH TRIALS 7

LIFE WITH TEMPTATIONS 21

LOSING YOUR JOB 31

LOSING A LOVED ONE 41

BREAKING UP 51

LOSING YOUR FAITH 61

LIFE RESTORATION 71

LIVING A FULFILLING LIFE 81

CONCLUSION 89

INTRODUCTION

Any broken part in your life is restored by God
but you need to understand
His ways to find favour

Revealed Ways of God

INTRODUCTION

The struggles of life have been with mankind since from the time when Adam and Eve fell into sin, to this day life is not always easy and comfortable for God's children. In the beginning, God created mankind in His image with a sole purpose for us to live a good and comfortable life as His sons and daughters.

God's desire was for us to love Him as our heavenly Father, to walk with Him and have fellowship with Him. Adam and Eve enjoyed having the fellowship with God in the Garden of Eden until they fell into sin. After the fall to sin, mankind was separated from God. Henceforth, redemption was required for our salvation.

Jesus Christ died on our behalf for us to reconcile with God and become His children to glorify Him as our heavenly Father.

As sons and daughters of God, we desire to live a good and comfortable life, free from problems that cause us hurt and pain but due to the realities of life, we now and then find ourselves facing serious challenges.

Sometimes the challenges come as a result of our own mistakes, poor decisions, wrong choices or things just happen beyond our control without doing anything wrong. Amid those challenges, we might lose something valuable and come to a point of despair and get the feeling of giving up in life because we feel it is enough.

The great prophet of God, Elijah, once came to a point of despair when chased by Jezebel to kill him. He cried to God and said, "It is enough! Now, Lord take my life, for I am no better than my fathers!" Instead, God sent an angel that told him to arise and eat because the journey was too great for him. After eating what God had provisioned, he got his strength back and continued with his journey (1 Kings 19: 1-8).

You must not give up in life no matter how adverse the situation might look because your journey is too great. Every human being is on earth to serve a particular purpose according to God's design. He is always present to help whenever you face challenges but you need to know His ways to find favour.

The purpose of this book is to help you understand and recognise the ways of God, particularly, when facing trials, temptations, losing your job, death of a loved one, breaking up with a partner and losing your faith. You will be empowered to deal with the loss and allow God to restore your fulfilling life, full of peace and joy.

CHAPTER ONE

LIFE WITH TRIALS

Revealed Ways of God

1

Trials form an integral part of your journey in life. You need to pass the test to get a reward from our heavenly Father.

Trials come from God to test our faith. They come in many forms, normally in the form of an outside power beyond the individual's control. God would usually test His people to determine the level of their faith and trust they have in Him. He takes you through the fiery of the trial under His watch and control. He is always in charge of the situation.

> The trial you face might happen in such a way that it is taking the last valuable thing you have in life

For every trial that you go through and pass the test, there is a reward from our Heavenly Father.

Trial of losing a valuable treasure

Abraham was called by God to bless him to become a father of nations. He was very old and had no child. God promised to bless him with a child in order to multiply and become the father of the nations.

At an appropriate time, God returned and blessed him with a son, Isaac. When he was happy that he was blessed with the one and only son, God told him to sacrifice his son, Isaac. As the man of faith, he did not ask God what will happen about the promise of him becoming the father of nations. Naturally speaking, the death of Isaac would mean the non-fulfilment of the promise.

In the early hours of the morning, Abraham took his son to Mount Moriah intending to sacrifice him as per God's instruction.

After making all the preparations for the sacrifice, God immediately appeared through an angel and stopped Abraham from sacrificing Isaac. God revealed to Abraham that He was testing his faith and found him to be righteous. He then offered a ram for the sacrifice (Genesis 22:12-13).

God went as far as calling Abraham His friend because of his high level of faith. He was blessed abundantly and became the father of nations as he was promised. To this day, those who live by faith to Christ are children of Abraham and will inherit Abraham's blessings (Galatians 3:29).

The trial you face might happen in such a way that it is taking the last valuable thing you have in life. You will ask yourself many questions such as, "Why is this happening to me?", "What wrong did I do to deserve this?" "What will happen to my beautiful and comfortable life?" Only to find that you did nothing wrong, God is just testing your faith.

You only need to believe and trust Him, the trial shall come to pass and after passing the test, God will reward you and pour out His blessings, abundantly.

Trial of losing fortunes and own life

Job is one of the well-known men for believing and fearing God. He was living a very good and comfortable life with his family. God was so very much pleased with his high level of faith and fear in Him.

A conversation between God and Satan is recorded in the scripture whereby God engaged Satan if he has noticed Job, the man who fears and trust God. And the Lord said to Satan, "Have you considered my servant Job, that there is none like him on the earth, a blameless and upright man, who fears God and turns away from evil?" (Job 1:8).

Satan took the opportunity and conducted an evil work of trying to destroy the life of Job while God was watching. He lost his wealth and children. Nevertheless, Job was not shaken he stood firm on his faith and kept trusting God. He never lost his faith, instead, he said, "God has given and naked I came from my mother's womb, and naked shall I return. The Lord gave, and the Lord has taken away; blessed be the name of the Lord" (Job 1.21).

> In midst of the trial, Job lost fortunes and became sick like losing his own life

The suffering of Job got to another level when Satan caused him to get sick from toe to head with painful boils (Job 2:7).

However, he persistently believed that the Redeemer lives. Finally, he passed the test and Satan was disappointed after all his evil work of trying to destroy his life. God was very pleased with Job's disposition and for passing the test. He restored his fortunes to be more than what he had before (Job 42:12).

The life of Job gives a good lesson to comprehend that God knows everything that happens in your life. In the midst of trials, He is always in charge. The onus remains with you if you keep your faith and pass the test to get the reward from our heavenly Father.

In the fiery of trials, we're motivated by Apostle Paul by saying, "Our reward will be far greater than our suffering" (2 Corinthians 4:17).

A difficult test

I once experienced a very serious challenge in my life that needed a child-like faith to get out of the situation. It happened that for two months I had requested my sister to deposit money into my bank account in which car insurance monthly premiums were being debited. After three months from the month I had asked her to deposit the money, my car was involved in an accident and it was written-off.

I approached my insurer to submit a claim and to my surprise, I was told that my insurance cover lapsed midnight and the car accident happened around 02.30. Just two hours after the insurance cover lapsed. This became a mystery for such timing.

Furthermore, the insurance consultant informed me,
"For two months we did not receive the premiums and one month was granted as a period of grace."

By the time the period of grace lapsed at midnight, the accident happened immediately at 02:30. It became explicit clear that I was engaging into a spiritual battle and my faith was going to be tested.

My heart in the joy of the Spirit burst into church hymn taken from the book of Psalm 91:1,

"He who dwells in the secret place of the Most High shall abide under the shadow of the Almighty. I will say of the LORD, He is my refuge and my fortress; My God, in Him I will trust."

I then went home to enquire from my sister as to what exactly happened to my request of her to make the deposits for two months since the insurance cover had lapsed due to non–payment. She told me,

"I made the deposits as you had requested."

She presented the deposit slips as proof. To our surprise, she had deposited to an incorrect bank account which meant indeed there were insufficient funds in my account to cover those premiums.

It then made sense why the insurance cover lapsed. Knowing how difficult the insurance claims could be and in my case, it was very clear that there were no premiums for two months.

The following day, I went to meet a branch manager of the insurance company to explain the situation and presented the deposit slips that I intended to deposit the money for my insurance premiums but selected an incorrect account.

The branch manager was very kind and helpful. In the back of my mind, I knew she was no longer in charge of the situation but God was. She said,

"Please write a memo to state what exactly happened and attach the deposit slips. I'm not promising anything; the headquarters will decide."

After submitting the memo with a heavy heart, I said to God,

"I have done the part that is possible for man. The next step is beyond my control and only you heavenly Father who will take over and deliver the outcome according to your will."

I waited for the outcome of my submission. The faithful day came after three weeks when I received a call from the insurance consultant. At that moment my heart was very heavy knowing that I would probably get the outcome of my submission as either declined or approved. As I was thinking deeply about how the impact would be if declined, knowing how much God loves me, I had the confidence that the outcome would be positive. The consultant broke the good news,

"The insurance cover has been reinstated and we will proceed with the claim."

I immediately gave thanks to our Almighty Gracious God and praised Him without ceasing. They proceeded with the claim and indeed it was successful.

The insurer settled the outstanding amount which I was supposed to pay for the next four years without having a car and they gave me cash back from a deposit cover which I was not even aware that it existed.

After the claim, I was approached by a senior manager at work who was selling a very beautiful, immaculate car that was never in my mind due to affordability at that time. He was selling the car for a very less price which one could not imagine in that condition. I indicated to him that I did have the interest to buy the car.

Since it was December period and he was ready to go on leave, he just handed over the car to me without applying for finance from the bank and he said,

"Enjoy Christmas driving the car, we'll see everything next year when I'm back from leave."

I could not believe it but it was really happening. I then realised that God was rewarding me for being steadfast on my faith and trusting Him during my trying times. God is very faithful and has no shadow of turning. He fulfils all His promises, all the time.

Trusting God in the midst of trials

Facing trials is very challenging but knowing that they are from our heavenly Father to test us, gives a bit of relief. We know that He loves us dearly and His main purpose with trials is to test our faith and reward us afterwards.

Sometimes even learners find it challenging when sitting for their exams, no matter how hard they have studied. It is not always pleasant to be tested but in the end, they express so much happiness when receiving the results with a pass.

> In the midst of trials be steadfast on your faith and trust God about everything

Apostle Peter says, "Beloved, do not think it strange concerning the fiery trial which is to try you, as though some strange things happened to you" (1 Peter 4:12).

As much as trials are unpleasant in their nature, they will always be part of your life. The knowledge and understanding that they're from God will help you to better respond when tested. You need to take it easy and think about a Father testing his beloved son or daughter.

In the midst of trials be steadfast on your faith and trust God about everything, even though certain things won't make sense.

Sometimes even some family members and friends might think the situation is too enormous to handle or severe to overcome but hold on, trusting God until you pass the test and He will surely reward you.

Revealed Ways of God 20

CHAPTER TWO

LIFE WITH TEMPTATIONS

Revealed Ways of God 22

2

Temptations form an integral part of your journey in life. You need to resist to find favour from our heavenly Father.

Temptations come from our internal desires. As human beings, we do have natural and pure desires. However, the principle is that those desires must be fulfilled in a manner that is acceptable to God. Satan normally tempts us to get the desires fulfilled in a manner that is not acceptable by our heavenly Father.

If we fail to control the desires to be fulfilled the godly way, we then allow Satan to lure us to fall into sin. The power of sin is on its promise for immediate gratification.

Over the years, I had learned that those who make offers, promise immediate fulfilment by saying, "You will get it right now", and I needed to be vigilant.

We have now learned that temptations are not from God but evil in nature and seek to break you down or take things away. According to the book of James 1:13, "God does not tempt anyone with evil because He cannot also be tempted with evil."

I got an insight about four basic steps to better understand how mankind get tempted and fall into sin. The steps can be framed with the following four D's; Desire, Deception, Disobedience and Death. I will apply the four basic steps when looking at how Adam and Eve were tempted and fell into sin while in the Garden of Eden.

Temptation steps

The application of the four D's in the temptation of Adam and Eve is as follows;

Desire – "Every man is tempted according to his desire" (James 1:14). Adam and Eve had a desire to gain wisdom hence they were tempted to eat from the fruit of the tree prohibited by God (Genesis 3:6).

The desire to have wisdom is natural and pure, and it's acceptable to have good desires but how they pursued to attain it was against the will of God.

Deception - When God instructed Adam and Eve not to eat the prohibited fruit, He told them, "Surely you will die." Satan deceived them using some of the words that were used by God but changed them for the deception by saying, "Surely you will not die."

Disobedience - Adam and Eve disobeyed God after eating the prohibited fruit He had instructed them not to eat. As a result, they fell into sin and God extremely hates sin. Because of His mercy and endless love. God made garments using animal skins for Adam and Eve, after seeing themselves being naked.

Death – God warned Adam and Eve about the consequence of falling into sin, "But you must not eat from the tree of the knowledge of good and evil, for when you eat from it, you will surely die" (Genesis 2:17). This is how the wages of sin became death. Since the fall of Adam and Eve to sin, all mankind is born in sin. Consequently, Jesus Christ died on our behalf for us to be saved.

Adam and Eve fell into temptation and sinned against God. Their fall was as a result of a desire they failed to control and pursued ungodly way to satisfy it.

Moreover, they allowed the version of Satan's word to supersede God's word hence they succumbed to deception.

The consequence was very much severe, death took effect as a wage of sin, and they lost the privilege and comfort of living in the Garden of Eden. Something precious was taken away from them.

As much as God loved them so dearly, He did not change His commandment to accommodate them, however, He gave Adam and Eve garments to show that He is Love and He cares. God is forever righteous and consistent with His declarations. We must always strive to obey His commandments and we'll find His favour.

The One who never sinned

Our Lord Jesus Christ was not spared from the temptations. After receiving baptism; He was led by the Holy Spirit to the wilderness to be tempted by Satan. After He fasted for forty days and forty nights, He was hungry and had the desire for food. Satan tested Him by asking that He changes the stones into loaves of bread (Mathew 4:3).

Jesus defeated Satan by not falling into the temptation. He controlled the desire for food after so much hunger. He said, "A man shall not live by bread alone but also with the word of God" (Mathew 4:4). He further refused to take instructions from Satan, no matter how convincing he was with his deception.

Our Lord Jesus Christ was tempted with all evil but He never sinned

---

God was very pleased with His Son, Jesus Christ, defeating Satan and the angels attended Him (Mathew 4:11).

After the temptations, Christ had clearly demonstrated that He was fit and worthy enough to undertake the mission of salvation for mankind.

Escaping temptation

In some years back, I was busy with my own project. The project came under a financial constraint to continue and I got stuck for a while. I had a desire for money to complete the project when suddenly,

I received a call from someone I had not talked to for a while, and I was really surprised. He said,

"Mr Mashego I need to offer you some help of making extra cash every month, and I'll do whatever work needed to be done to generate the income. You'll receive the money monthly in your bank account. You will have to thank me afterwards."

I listened carefully to understand the means of generating the extra cash and realised it was against my principles. I vehemently rejected the offer knowing that it would not be according to the will of God. I controlled my desire for money that I needed for the project, not to allow Satan to lure me into sin.

I said the project can delay than fulfilling my desire in a manner that was not acceptable to God. I then refused to accept his convincing words. Surprisingly, the month after receiving that call and offer from that person, I received my salary doubled. I could not hold back my happiness, my heart was jumping up and down inside me. I immediately enquired from work as to what the money was for. I was told it was my back pay for some of my long overdue allowances. I said,

"Oh thank you, Lord. You're good all the time and let your name be praised."

> **Always try to make it a principle that your desires are fulfilled in a manner that is acceptable to God**

The money just came at the right time when I really needed it. I completed my project happily and peaceful in a manner that was acceptable to our heavenly Father.

Resisting temptations

Apostle Paul says, "No temptation has overtaken you that is not common to man. God is faithful and He will not let you be tempted beyond your ability but with the temptation, He will also provide the way of escape, that you may be able to endure it" (1 Corinthians 10:13).

Since you're tempted according to your internal desires, the word says, "Above all else, guard your heart, for everything you do flows from it (Proverbs 4:23). Do not accept any version of the word that is not aligned with God's word. Always make it a principle that your desires are fulfilled in a manner that is acceptable to God.

After resisting Satan, he will flee from you and the angels of God will come and attend to you as they did to our Lord Jesus Christ.

We have this beautiful hymn that is commonly known, "What a Friend we have in Jesus." (Joseph Scriven, 1820-1885). He is always present to help you when you are facing trials and temptations.

Have we trials and temptations?
Is there trouble anywhere?
We should never be discouraged
Take it to the Lord in prayer

To resist temptations, you need to guard the desires of your heart and be firm on the version of the truth from God's word, you will then find God's favour. In the midst of trials and temptations, you can lose something very valuable.

There're other three unbearable and painful losses you may face in life that could break your heart and crush the spirit; losing your job, death of a loved one, and a breakup. These three losses will be covered extensively in the next chapters.

CHAPTER THREE

LOSING YOUR JOB

3

God provides during trying times and He makes a way in the wilderness

Every person needs a source of income for a better life. Losing your job is one of the most stressful situations a person can experience in their adult life. Unfortunately, there are circumstances in life beyond your control that cause you to lose your job. During the dreadful loss, God's provision will always be there to carry you through and makes a way for you to move forward.

The Lord cares

Our Lord Jesus says, "Therefore, I tell you, do not be anxious about your life, what you will eat or what you will drink, nor about your body, what will you put on. Is not life more than food, and the body more than clothing? Look at the birds of the air: they neither sow nor reap nor gather into barns, and yet your heavenly Father feeds them" (Mathew 6:28).

God always care about what we have to eat and wear. He fed the Israelites with manna when there was no food and He made garments for Adam and Eve to wear after they fell into sin and left the Garden of Eden. He won't give you the same manna and garments today but He'll provide you with any other means possible according to His will.

In the book of Jeremiah 39:18, God says, "For I will surely save you, and you shall not fall by the sword, but you shall have your life as a prize of war because you have put your trust in me, declares the Lord." Our loving heavenly Father is forever present in our lives to provide during trying times.

God is forever faithful only if we put trust in Him. Surrender your situation with faith and fervent prayer to ask for help and He will surely intervene.

The Lord provides and makes a way

After serving many years in one of the companies that I worked for, I decided it was time to quit and pursue other avenues. My boss who was in tears over my departure tried to give me a counteroffer. She said,

"Hezekiel, it is not easy to let you go, and I have thought the best thing I can do is to give you a counteroffer."

I said, *"It is not really about money that I'm leaving but to explore other avenues building my career."*

I left to join a new company and when I was about to conclude two years serving the company, we were given a one- month notice that our project was closing down. As someone who knows the ways of God, I did not panic and was never moved by the bad news. My boss even asked me,

"Why do you seem like you're not shaken by this bad news?"

I smiled and I said, *"All is well in my soul."*

The last day we had a farewell function, I posted on my Facebook page saying I was going on a long leave, and instead of saying I will be unemployed.

I carried this message deep in my heart saying, I'm on long leave and with a firm belief that God will intervene soon.

I attended an interview just after three weeks of losing my job. I had the confidence as I always have that I will get the job and hoping there won't be much financial impact due to the job loss. I waited long enough without getting any feedback from the company. I followed up via email and did not get a reply. I then realised the outcome of the interview was negative.

I tried setting up a business hoping that since I had more time to focus, things will work out. It was very challenging to get things moving as I expected and in actual fact, it was the business that was causing me even much more stress. I did not make any profit from the capital injected, instead, I made a loss.

I stayed at home for five months without a job and without cashing up any pension benefits. I had debts and bills to pay, however, life was not a serious struggle with the provisioning of God. The family never experienced any shortage of basics needs. I was even managing to pay little car instalments and taking long trips like someone who was working.

The living God that we serve will always provide. He will bring people in your life you never thought of helping you. There will be other sources of money that will be opened to sustain you. He fed the prophet, Elijah, through the ravens and He will also feed you in any way according to His will.

Trust God in these challenging times and know that the fountain of the provision is opened for you. Eat and arise because your journey of life is great.

While still waiting on the Lord to show me a way to go, a friend of mine forwarded me a job advert. It was a company that I never thought I would get a job from since there was no hiring taking place at the time but only for very critical and scarce skills positions that could be motivated and justified.

I applied for the advertised position and was invited for an interview. The process to conclude my appointment was the shortest I have ever experienced in my lifetime. Finally, after five months of being unemployed, I got an offer in a company where there was a moratorium on hiring, the CEO of the company had to personally approve my appointment.

When God opens a door for you, no one will close it and when He shuts it, no one will open it. What is not possible with man is always possible with God.

God has the absolute power to make a way for you in a wilderness.

The offer was for a twelve months' contract but still, I was never worried knowing my God is always at work for me to serve His purpose. My contract was renewed without any challenges just before the twelve months ended.

I attended an interview for a permanent position in another company and when I was about to be appointed, that company too, imposed a moratorium on hiring.

Knowing that my Redeemer lives, I was not worried but remained still waiting on the Lord to lead me on the way to follow. Every answer that comes from Him is Amen. After six months waiting joyfully on the Lord, the moratorium was lifted and I was permanently employed.

God makes a way

The book of Proverbs states that "Trust in the Lord with all your heart and do not lean on your own understanding. In all your ways acknowledge Him, and He will make straight your paths," (Proverbs 3:5-6).

Furthermore, the prophet Isaiah says, "You need to put behind what has happened and look forward to the new things that the Lord will do for you. He will make a way in the wilderness and rivers in the desert" (Isaiah 43:18-19).

God will make a way for you in the wilderness and rivers in the desert

---

God made a way for Lot and his family to move out of the City of Sodom before destruction. He gave them a clear instruction not to look back but one of his wives did look back. Unfortunately, she got stuck and never reached the place that God had destined for the family. Forget what is behind and look ahead to what God has prepared for you.

Apostle Paul is encouraging us with this word from Philippians 3:12, "I do not consider myself yet to have taken hold of it. But one thing I do: Forgetting what is behind and straining towards what is ahead."

God will always make a way for you and it does not matter how bad the situation might look. You just need to do your best and He will do the rest. He is good all the time and He fulfils all His promises.

CHAPTER FOUR

LOSING A LOVED ONE

4

To measure the level of pain of losing a loved one, look at how Our Lord Jesus reacted when He lost His friend Lazarus, nonetheless, there's comfort and hope

We are all born in this world and we know that at some point we shall die, however, death is the greatest enemy of mankind. The loss of a loved one causes so much pain and sorrow. To measure the level of such pain, you can look at how Our Lord Jesus reacted when He lost His friend, Lazarus. He was hit very hard by the death. The book of John 11:35 tells us that the Lord wept by the death of His friend, Lazarus.

Grieving with comfort and hope

My father was the first one to pass on in my family. Seven years later, my mother joined him in the realm of the departed. Just after three years, my eldest sister also departed to join our parents. While I was still grieving for my eldest sister, in just two years, my youngest sister who was the last born, passed on as well. After that, at least, I experienced a break for a while without losing a sibling then ten years later, my brother joined the family in the realm of the departed.

In the family of seven I have lost five family members, there are now only two of us left, my younger sister and me. The pains and sorrows that we had to go through were severe. The passing of my brother who became the fifth family member to depart created so much void and I got the deep feeling that my immediate family is no longer in this world.

Surely, we will not fully understand everything now but when we get to eternity our heavenly Father will reveal all the answers.

As part of God's provision, He has given me an amazingly supportive family, friends and brothers and sisters in Christ. The love and support that I have constantly experienced during those painful losses are extraordinary.

They're forever available and helping in the best way possible. This kind of love and care have really moved my soul. I've been praying fervently for them to receive God's blessings in a very special way.

The understanding and knowledge that God has revealed especially about our eternal future with Him and our loved ones in the realm of departed, is consistently giving me comfort and hope. You also need this comfort and hope for such unbearable painful loss.

Jesus our Comforter

Our Lord Jesus Christ died and lived to be the king of the dead and living (Romans 14:9). As a result, He's the only one who can give us complete comfort for the sorrow and hope for the future with our loved ones. At the transfiguration mountain, Our Lord Jesus Christ was with three living Apostles, Peter, James and John, suddenly Elijah and Moses who were long dead appeared, talking to Jesus (Matthew 17:1-3).

Before his death, Jesus promised one of the sinners crucified with Him that on the very same day He will be with him in paradise (Luke 23:43). Christ spoke with power and authority indicating that truly He is the son of God and He has power over death.

The Lord knows the pain of losing a loved one and He also knows the life of the dead in the realm of the departed both hades and paradise, and this knowledge must give you much comfort.

The below verse from a known hymn, "What a Friend we have in Jesus," (Joseph Scriven, 1820 -1885) assures us that we have a good Friend in Jesus, who's very faithful and shares our sorrows. You need to take everything to Him in prayer.

Hymn: What a Friend we have in Jesus

Can we find a friend so faithful
who will all our sorrows share?
Jesus knows our every weakness
Take it to the Lord in prayer

Home for the departed

Since we build a home for our physical body there is also the home for our spiritual body in the beyond. Apostle Paul gives us comfort according to what is written in 2 Corinthians 5:1, "We know that if our earthly tent is destroyed, we have a building of God, a house not built with hands, eternal in the heavens." This home is built by God where His love and peace abide, there is no more pain nor suffering and distress.

The below beautiful hymn also gives us an insight about this spiritual home. "O the home of my soul is on high" (De Witt Huntington, 1830-1912).

Oh the home of my soul is on high,
far beyond every sorrow and sigh,
where the numberless,
sanctified fold praised God with a joy that's untold

As you know the beauty of nature that God has created, we go as far as travelling around the world seeing this beautiful nature. God is absolutely perfect in everything that He's doing. Can you imagine the beauty of the spiritual home built by Him? Indeed, our loved ones are in a far better place than any other place we have ever known.

The below beautiful hymnal verse also attests about this beautiful home for the departed: Hymn: "Beyond, where no more clouds appear". (George C Stebbins, 1846-1945).

Beyond, where no more clouds appear,
No night the world enshrouds,
a mansion's there prepared for me,
Where naught my longing clouds

Furthermore, our loved ones are getting rest from the hardship they might have been experiencing in their lives.

According to the book of Revelation 14:13, "...Blessed are the dead which die in the Lord from now on: Yes, said the Spirit that they may rest from their labours; and their works do follow them".

This knowledge about the spiritual beautiful home must also give you comfort knowing that your loved ones are living comfortable and resting in peace.

Reunion

The most joyful comfort that we receive regarding the loved ones in the beyond is the belief that one day we shall re-unite with them. The joy on that day will be beyond measure and not comparable with any joy that you might have ever experienced in your lifetime. The joy will last forever since there will be no more separation. We shall be with the Lord and our loved ones forever.

Apostle Paul says, "We must have knowledge about the departed so that our grief is not like those who do not have hope. When Christ returns, He will raise them first and we shall be changed and taken as well so that we will be with the Lord forever" (1 Thessalonians 4:13-17).

You're temporarily separated from your loved ones since you're living in flesh and they're living in spirit.

Always have comfort and keep the hope alive that one day you shall reunite with your loved ones from the beyond forever.

CHAPTER FIVE

BREAKING UP

5

One of the most painful parts of a breakup is that it ends what you have come to know, the familiar is gone and plans have changed

We are born and grow up within a family that God has chosen for us to belong by blood. When we are grown up there comes a time to choose a partner. In that relationship of choice, we invest love and emotions to keep it alive. We also make a lot of sacrifices driven by the love for our partner. An ideal relationship is to exist until death separates the couples.

Breaking up

Unfortunately, there are times when a relationship suffers and leads to a breakup. In most cases, the breakup occurs while love still exists in the relationship. It might happen that one party is committing grievous mistakes that are obviously unacceptable to the other. These mistakes will often cause conflicts, hurt and pain.

The mind of the one who is always offended will reason that it's better to quit for peace sake but the heart might not easily detach because there is still love burning. If parties fail to align and create a happy and healthy relationship, the relationship will finally end up dying. In this instance, the relationship did not experience a natural death but it was killed due to unacceptable behaviours.

> **In most cases, the breakup occurs while love still exists in a relationship**

The death of a relationship brings so much pain to both parties. It becomes a pain that can be likened to losing a loved one due to death. It feels like the world has stopped moving and everything has come to a complete stop. Others get severely affected by a breakup in such a way that they even get depressed and require serious intervention.

One of the most painful parts of a breakup is that it ends what you have come to know for some time, what used to be familiar is gone and plans have to change. The future, all of a sudden, seems to have changed to a different direction.

The Lord says, "For I hate divorce" (Malachi 2:16). True, it causes so much hurt and pain to the couples, children, family and friends. The life of the family that used to be intact gets disintegrated. Well, after it happened for whatever reasons, we still need our loving and caring heavenly Father to heal the broken hearts. We need God to help the family members to continue living a good and comfortable life even though they're no longer together.

Receiving-end of a breakup

If you're the party on the receiving end of a breakup, you might feel angry, rejected or betrayed. You feel physically ill, exhausted, and devastated. However, our heavenly Father will wipe your tears and heal your broken heart. "The Lord is near to the broken-hearted and saves the crushed in Spirit," (Psalm 34:18).

If you have committed a mistake that led to the end of a relationship, you'll feel guilty and shameful, nevertheless, you don't need to be too hard on yourself for too long.

Humans are fallible by nature, you will now and then stumble. Every time you fall, you must wake up and move forward in order to get your life restored and fulfilling.

King David committed a grievous mistake by having an affair with Bathsheba that led to the death of her husband Uriah (2 Samuel 11). The king regretted his actions and showed remorse to God and he was forgiven.

Practical steps to deal with a mistake

I recommend the following basic steps that can help you to practically deal with the mistake you might have committed that caused the breakup of your relationship:
1) Acknowledge the mistake, knowing that you're a human being, you are not perfect, and forgive yourself.
2) Take responsibility for your actions, don't shift the blame to someone else.
3) Apologise to those you might have hurt.
4) Improve from the lesson learned.

God will always forgive if you show remorse. According to the book of 1 John 1:9, "If we confess our sins, He is faithful and just to forgive us our sins and to cleanse us from all unrighteousness."

Healing from the breakup

After the breakup, you need some time to heal, it's not ideal to quickly jump into another relationship. The hurt and pain from a previous relationship are likely to affect the next one if healing did not take place. Your next partner might have high expectations that you're not going to be able to meet with a bleeding heart from the breakup.

The painful part is when the new partner loses patience with you and fails to afford you more time to heal properly. In the process, your new partner might get hurt, lose patience and focus. The person who is supposed to love, care and support you, could be the one now hurting you and getting your heart even more shattered and your spirit completely crushed.

It's important not to rush things – it's your time to reset, recharge and draw wisdom from the experience. It is an important part of rebuilding and strengthening the sense of who you are, outside the relationship. Therapists do recommend different mechanisms to help you heal from a breakup. I also recommend the following basic steps that can help you with the healing process:

1) **Let yourself grief**

When you feel pain from a loss, allowing yourself time to grieve is one of the most important steps in the healing process.

2) **Talk to supportive people**

Talking to a trusted family member or a friend can help you. You do need someone to listen in order to ventilate your hurt and pain. You may decide to consult for professional help from therapists and that may be more appropriate or useful.

3) **Eat and sleep**

When the breakup strikes, it's possible to lose your eating and sleeping patterns. As difficult as it may be, it's the most crucial time to stick to good eating and sleeping patterns.

4) **Forgive**

Forgive yourself and the other person to be emotionally and mentally free. Learn and grow from this bad experience. Stop blaming, instead, liberate yourself.

5) **Reclaim yourself**

This is the most important stage where you have to recover and reclaim your life outside the relationship. Bring together the parts of yourself that might have been pushed aside during the relationship.

After the discovery of those parts, find ways to rebuild them and nurture them. More and above the prescribed and recommended mechanisms to deal with the breakup, you definitely need God to perfect the healing.

> The hurt and pain from a previous relationship are likely to affect the next one if healing did not take place

Any broken part of your life is fully restored by God. He has created you and knows you much better than any other person who might try to offer help to fix what is broken and missing in your life.

Keep praying to God for the healing of your broken heart and meditate on the word. After healing has properly taken place, you still need to seek guidance from God to direct you about the next path to follow.

CHAPTER SIX

LOSING YOUR FAITH

6

Losing faith is to stop trusting God,

when facing trials, temptations

and other challenges in life.

"Faith is the substance of things hoped for, the evidence of things not seen," (Hebrew 11:1). It is the connecting power into the spiritual realm, which links us to God. "Faith comes by hearing and hearing by the Word of God" (Romans 10:17). He expects us to live by faith to please Him as our heavenly Father.

Conversely, losing faith is to stop trusting God when facing trials, temptations and other challenges in life. The loss of faith can also be caused by waiting too long on the Lord to change an adverse situation. Abraham and Sarah waited for a long time for their son, Isaac to be born after God had promised until Sarah decided that Abraham must have a child with a servant, Hagar. As a result, Ishmael was born.

After the birth of Ishmael, God fulfilled His promise by blessing Abraham and Sarah with the son. He's always righteous and faithful to His promises. Apostle Paul attests this in 2 Corinthians 1:20 "For all the promises of God in Him are yes, and in Him Amen, to the glory of God through us."

Sadly, after the birth of Isaac, the promised child by God a conflict erupted between Sarah and Hagar. Sarah, the one who had recommended the backup plan to get an heir from Hagar changed the tune after her son, Isaac, was born. Unfortunately, Hagar and her son, Ishmael, were forced to leave Abraham's household (Genesis 21:8-14). Sometimes we cause unnecessary problems by trying to overtake God when He's still at work to fulfil a promise. If Abraham and Sarah waited patiently on God this problem would not have existed.

We can also learn about the loss of faith when Job was facing trials in his life. His wife lost faith that the situation was going to change. She said it's better for Job to curse God and die once (Job 2:9). She did not see God coming to intervene and she completely lost her faith.

God's timing

Naturally, when we desire for something to happen, our main challenge is waiting for a long time. We expect things to happen quicker. Most of the time we set our timelines hoping to achieve as soon as possible. We get disappointed when our timing come to pass and nothing had happened. God's timing cannot be estimated nor understood. His timing is completely different from ours.

> God's timing cannot be estimated nor understood

- Abraham and Sarah had their own expectation hoping the promise of the child would be fulfilled quicker, hence they lost patience after realising it was taking long. It took them twenty-five years to get their child after the promise (Genesis 12:1-4 & Genesis 21:1-5).

- It took Joseph thirteen years to become the Prime Minister of Egypt after God appeared to him in a dream when he was seventeen years old (Genesis 37:1-9 & Genesis 41:46).

- The Holy Spirit came on Pentecost ten days after Jesus's ascension to fulfil the promise He made to His Apostles (Acts 1:8 & Acts 2:1-4).

In all these different timings either long or short, God was always on time. He declares the end in the beginning, and does everything according to His pleasure. His will shall always stand.

No matter how long you have waited on the Lord to fulfil the promise or change your situation, you must not lose faith. Keep on believing and trusting God even if it does not make sense any more. At an appropriate time, He will appear.

Leaving the matter in God's hands

In one of the organizations that I once worked for, I experienced a very serious delay in getting appointed to a higher position though I was meeting all the requirements. Some of my colleagues were appointed without challenges. When making follow-ups, Human Resources (HR) would state reasons that were so much confusing.

The feedback was always about something that needed to be fixed on the system before I could be appointed but no one really understood what needed to be done. I followed up until I got tired and handed over to God to fight the battle.

The management from my region constantly contacted our headquarters requesting them to fix the problem but it dragged for years and years not being resolved.

One day I went to a senior manager's office to present some documents for a signature. He said to me,

"I see all your colleagues have been appointed to higher positions but only you are still left behind." He further said,

"What surprises me is that you're always positive, smiling and working diligently."

He assured me that they were doing their best to get the matter resolved. I thanked him and in my heart, I said, my Redeemer lives, it does not matter how long it takes but I know that this matter is now in God's hands and at an appropriate time He will return, and the benefits that seem to be lost will be compensated.

> I knew the matter was in God's hands, and at an appropriate time, He will return

Indeed, God appeared at an appropriate time. While I was still waiting for the appointment, another position higher than the one I was waiting for, was advertised. I applied and was appointed without many challenges.

I knew that it was God's reward for not losing faith in Him. The new position offered was a good stepping stone for achieving my aspiration. After one year, I completely moved to a new direction in my career that I had been aspiring and praying for some time.

God intervenes

A paralysed man had been coming to the pool of Bethesda for thirty-eight years still having a living faith that one day he was going to get healed. What we learn from the scripture is that an angel was stirring the pool every day in the morning. Any person who had ailments or sickness had to go in first to receive healing. The paralysed man needed someone to help him go in first after the angel had stirred the pool. Imagine for such faith, so many years but still believing that one day the situation would change.

Indeed, finally, the situation changed in a way that he never expected. As he was expecting an ordinary person to help him. Our Lord Jesus Christ appeared and intervened, the man was finally healed (John 5:5-8).

Keep on believing and trusting God even if it does not make sense any more

When Lazarus was sick, his sisters sent a message to Jesus to come home and help. He came after four days after he had died and buried. The faith was lost; the family did not think there was anything Jesus could do. Surprisingly, He raised him from the death (John 11:44).

When they thought it was too late Our Lord Jesus Christ was still on time, God's timing cannot be estimated or understood. You must always keep your child-like faith and know that He is always in control of all situations. God is never late but always on time. At an appropriate time, He will finally appear to change the situation.

CHAPTER SEVEN

LIFE RESTORATION

7

The good news is that God is also known as the God of restoration. Whatever is lost in your life can be restored according to His will

The previous chapters have extensively covered different agonizing and painful losses a person can experience in a lifetime. Some go as far as losing their faith and give up in life. The good news is that God is also known as the God of restoration. Whatever is lost in your life can be restored according to His will.

The book of Luke 22: 50-51 tells us that during the arrest of Jesus, one of His disciples, Simon Peter, drew his sword and struck the servant of the high priest, cutting off his right ear. Jesus touched the man's ear and healed him. The ear was fully restored and got back to its original condition. This was another illustration that God has the power to restore what is lost in our lives and again live a normal fulfilling life.

In the book of Isaiah God says, "Do not remember the former things, nor consider the things of old. Behold, I will do a new thing, now it shall spring forth; shall you not know it? I will even make a road in the wilderness and rivers in the desert" (Isaiah 43:18-19). The story of Job gives us good testimony regarding God's restoration.

Therefore, you need to be joyful and praising "my Redeemer lives" and keep believing that at an appropriate time, God will restore whatever is lost.

According to the book of Jeremiah 29:11, God says, "I know the plans I have for you, declares the Lord, plans to prosper you." Our Lord Jesus Christ says, "So don't worry about tomorrow" (Mathew 6:34). God does take care of your plans and the future.

Letting God direct your steps

A man plans his ways and God directs his steps (Proverbs 16:9). It is not always easy to be still and in peace waiting on the Lord. Sometimes doubt comes as a result of impatience and trusting too much in your ability to direct your own steps.

Lot directed his steps - When there was a quarrel amongst the shepherds of Abraham and Lot, Abraham advised Lot that it would be better they separated ways so they could have peace since their shepherds were fighting over a grazing land.

He then offered Lot an opportunity to choose where to go. Lot did not enquire from God to direct his steps, instead, he chose a green fertile land he saw in the east. Unfortunately, the city that he chose was Sodom that was subsequently destroyed (Genesis 19:1-16).

Abraham asked God to direct his steps - Abraham asked God to direct the steps of his servant Eliezer on his assigned task to search a wife for his son, Isaac. Abraham believed that God was going to lead the way. He told his servant, Eliezer that, "He will send His angel ahead of you and He will see to it that you find a wife there for my son" (Genesis 24:7).

Eliezer turned to God and made the following prayer

"O Lord God of my master Abraham, please give me success this day, and show kindness to my master Abraham.
Behold, here I stand by the well of water, and the daughters of the men of the city are coming out to draw water.
Now let it be that the young woman to whom I say, 'Please let down your pitcher that I may drink,' and she says, 'Drink, and I will also give your camels a drink'— let her be the one You have appointed for Your servant Isaac. And by this, I will know that you have shown kindness to my master" (Genesis 24:12 -14).

Before He could finish his prayer, Rebekah approached and he asked her for water. She responded exactly according to the sign that He had set. Eliezer was convinced that she was the one for Isaac.

Indeed, she was the one, she fell within the category that Abraham himself had desired. You need to put your plans in God's hands. He'll direct your steps in the right direction to get your life restored.

Exercising Child-like faith

You need to act in a childlike faith that produces tangible results in order to get your life restored.
When acting in childlike faith, you put aside your experience, knowledge and understanding regarding the laws of nature. You believe that what is not possible with man is possible with God.

Some disciples of Christ had adequate experience in fishing. The Lord Jesus approached in the morning and instructed them to put their nets exactly where they've been toiling the whole night but could not catch anything. Simon said to Him, "We have toiled all the night and have taken nothing. Yet at your word I will let down the net, and doing this they enclosed a multitude of fish," (Luke 5:4-6). The disciples had to disregard their experience and skill of fishing to allow the power of God to work.

You need to believe and trust God in a child-like faith in order to allow Him to do wonders in your life. Sometimes it is very easy under normal circumstances to say we trust God. But when the trials, temptations and other challenges take place, our trust in Him can get shaken, therefore, you need to stand firm and keep trusting Him.

A child always believes that his/her father or mother can overcome any challenging situation. Shadrack, Meshack & Abednego demonstrated a child-like faith by telling Nebuchadnezzar that our God in whom we believe, shall deliver us from this fiery of fire. Trust God in all situations, He will deliver you and restore what is lost.

The power of God

God is able to fast track your life and make it far better than you have ever thought within a short time. He does things according to His plan and will. God's power operates beyond the laws of nature.

> God exists outside space and time, He's able to fast track whatever is needed in your life

The book of Ephesians 3:20 says, "Now to Him who is able to do immeasurably more than all we ask or imagine, according to His power that is at work within us."

For our understanding, the power of God is amazingly stated in the book of Job 26:7-14,

"He stretches out the north over empty space; He hangs the earth on nothing.

He binds up the water in His thick clouds, yet the clouds are not broken under it.

He covers the face of His throne and spreads His cloud over it.

"He drew a circular horizon on the face of the waters at the boundary of light and darkness.

The pillars of heaven tremble, and are astonished at His rebuke.

He stirs up the sea with His power, and by His understanding He breaks up the storm.

By His Spirit He adorned the heavens His hand pierced the fleeing serpent.

Indeed, these are the mere edges of His ways, and how small a whisper we hear of Him! But the thunder of His power who can understand?"

Truly, God is Almighty and Powerful, you only need faith to invite His power to work in your life and restores what is lost.

Transformation

Butterflies are considered as one of the beautiful creatures in the world. They undergo a transformation process that includes being locked inside a cocoon for several days. After a certain number of days, they come out of the cocoon having transformed to be this beautiful butterfly. They always remind us that there can be beauty at the end of all pain, you need to allow God to transform the pain into gain.

Our heavenly Father is the one who can transform and restore you to attain your beautiful and comfortable fulfilling life.

The book of Psalms 51:10-12 says, "Create in me a pure heart, O God, and renew a steadfast spirit within me. Do not cast me from your presence or take your Holy Spirit from me. Restore to me the joy of your salvation and grant me a willing spirit, to sustain me."

> Butterflies remind us that there can be beauty at the end of all pain

After experiencing the trials, temptations, losing your job, pain of losing a loved one due to death, pain from a breakup and losing your faith, there is still a beautiful life afterwards. Your good and comfortable life can be restored to be a fulfilling one by our loving, caring and gracious heavenly Father.

CHAPTER EIGHT

LIVING A FULFILLING LIFE

8

A fulfilling life comes after a process of going through challenges, failures and victories.

A fulfilling life comes after a process of going through challenges, failures and victories. At this stage of the fulfilling life, you have developed a strong character to deal with most of the challenges. You have experienced God through the trials, temptations and painful loss. You speak with a strong conviction when you say my Redeemer lives and it's no longer a matter of just believing in God but knowing Him.

You're satisfied, content and happy with what God has done for you, moreover you're happy with life, and you're always joyful.

Happiness and Joy

We normally desire to be forever happy in life, unfortunately, this is not always possible, and however, we can always be joyful.

Happiness -depends on favourable situations, if something good happens then we become happy and in contrast, if something bad happens then we become unhappy. In this current life, there will be times when you are happy and unhappy, depending on the circumstances.

Joy -is like the sun that keeps shining even when the night falls and the clouds cover it. The world will not stop with its tribulations but you can always live with the peace of Christ and be joyful.

The peace of Christ does not mean the absence of trouble but the serene inside you that is in harmony with our heavenly Father.

The main reason that gives us joy is the conviction that God loves us as His children and His love is unconditional.

> The peace of Christ does not mean the absence of trouble but the serene inside you that is in harmony with our heavenly Father

Apostle Paul and Silas were singing and praising while in prison. Their freedom and dignity were taken away, nonetheless, the bars of the prison did not stop them from being joyful (Acts 16:25). The below beautiful hymnal verse attests to the reason for us to be forever joyful. "Let your hearts be ever joyful" (J A Reitz, 1838-1904.)

Let your hearts be ever joyful
and filled with gratitude and cheer,
for the Father kind in heaven
calls us all His children dear.

Remaining with God until the end

> Absolutely nothing shall separate me from the love of God

King David said, "One thing I have desired of the Lord, that will I seek: that I may dwell in the house of the Lord, this I will seek: to remain in the Lord's house all the days of my life". (Psalm: 27:4). Our Lord Jesus

Christ has also taught us to remain faithful and obedient to our heavenly Father until to the end.

You need to always live with the vow that absolutely nothing shall separate you from the love of God, neither by losing your job, the loved one due to death, nor the breakup.

Our treasure in heaven is far greater than the earthly one. Keep your treasure in heaven, a place where thieves cannot come to break and take away your wealth.

The goal of our faith is to be with our heavenly Father in eternity. The relationship with God starts now in our earthly life. This relationship will continue when we get to our heavenly home. If you keep your focus in seeking His kingdom, He'll provide you with the earthly needs since He knows all your needs.

The book of Mathew 6:33 says, "But seek first the kingdom of God and His righteousness, and all these things will be added to you."

In the journey of my faith, I came to a point of going beyond believing in God but knowing Him. If you know God's ways then you know Him.

Moses said to God, "…teach me your ways so I may know you and continue to find favour in you" (Exodus 33:13).

At the end of everyone's life on earth, people say last words about how they have known that person, moreover, when that person enters the realm of the departed the same words will also be spoken.

Our works on earth will always follow us. The book of Revelation 14:13 says, "And I heard a voice from heaven saying to me, "Write, Blessed are the dead which die in the Lord from now on!". Yes, said the Spirit, "that they may rest from their labours; and their works do follow them."

In the journey of my faith, I came to a point of going beyond believing in God but knowing Him

---

May you always strive to remain in the ways of God until to the end and the good works will follow you such as:

- "I have fought the good fight, I have finished the race, I have kept the faith, Finally, there is laid up for me the crown of righteousness, which the Lord, the righteous Judge, will give to me on that Day, and not to me only but also to all who have loved His appearing." (2 Timothy 4:7-8).

- "…Well done, good and faithful servant! you have been faithful with a few things,.."(Mathew 25:21).

- "...after he had served his own generation by the will of God, fell on sleep and was laid to his fathers..." (Acts 13:36).

CONCLUSION

God heals everything,
He restores what is lost
and you can live a fulfilling life.

CONCLUSION

As a human being, you'll face trials in the journey of life. Trials are the tests that come from God and you pass them by exercising faith and trust in Him. In the process of going through these trials, you may lose something valuable that will inflict pain. God heals the pain and rewards you if you were steadfast until the end of the trial.

Furthermore, temptations will also visit you now and then, they approach you through your internal desires. If you fail to control the internal desires, Satan has an opportunity to draw you into sin and satisfy your desires in a way that is not acceptable to God. When you surrender to the temptations, he'll break you or take away something.

To resist temptations, you need to guard your desires to ensure they're satisfied in a godly manner and always dwell on the version of the truth from God.

In this journey of life, there're three most painful losses that can break your heart and crush your spirit:
- Firstly, the pain of losing your job. God heals the pain, provides for your needs during the trying times and makes a way of restoring what is lost.

- Secondly, the loss of a loved one due to death. God heals this pain by providing comfort and hope for the future with the loved ones.

- Lastly, the pain of the breakup with your partner. God also heals the pain and you get an opportunity to reclaim yourself.

As a result of facing the trials, temptations and losses, you might end up losing your faith. Losing your faith can mainly be caused by waiting for too long on the Lord to appear. God's timing cannot be estimated nor understood but He's always on time. You need to keep trusting Him, waiting on Him and be patient. He'll finally appear at an appropriate time.

After God has appeared to heal the pain of trials, temptations and painful losses, He is also able to restore what is lost according to His will. You need to follow His ways to get favour from Him.

Finally, as a tried and tested child of God, you will live and experience a fulfilling joyful life and your life will continue further in eternity with our heavenly Father.

May the grace of the Lord Jesus Christ, the love of God, and the fellowship of the Holy Spirit be with you.
Amen.

www.ingramcontent.com/pod-product-compliance
Lightning Source LLC
Chambersburg PA
CBHW071408290426
44108CB00014B/1740